I0845474

Foraging for Gold in Appalachia: Tips for Hunting Chanterelles and Other Prized Mushrooms

Written by Carl E. Miller and Lily Jo White (in association with Ohio River Valley Mushroom Hunters)

This book does not recommend eating and/or selling wild mushrooms. This is for documentation and educational purposes only! Always use caution!

Foraging for wild mushrooms can prove to be a true challenge, with seemingly the best hunters being extremely tight-lipped about where exactly you can look to find the most prized fungi. In this book, I will highlight some of these precious areas where they grow— with the main focus being on Chanterelle mushrooms (genera; Cantharellus, Craterellus, Gomphus, and Polyozellus), which are constantly ranked on the top ten most expensive wild mushrooms lists.

Although the primary focus of this book will be on hunting for Chanterelles, I will also cover plenty of other tips for foraging for many other prized mushrooms, such as; Chicken-of-the-woods, Hen-of-the-woods, Shrimp-of-the-woods, Old-Man-of-the-woods, Oysters, Honey mushrooms, Morels, Amanita muscaria and more…

So, despite the long history of mushroom hunters being secretive, it's finally time to discuss some of these professional tips and look at what makes for a perfect fungi habitat. Before you begin foraging, it's always wise to know what you're looking for exactly and be prepared for certain species, and let the others be a surprise.

Now, you can have several different mushroom types in mind, but it's best to at least have a good visualization of what you're looking for. So before you head out, perhaps look at what's in season and research some images for a while. This alone will make spotting the mushrooms easier, simply because you've already trained your eyes to look at them.

Some people who hunt for Morels even attach their first find to their walking stick, essentially training their mind to spot it and making it easier to find others as they walk. It's also best to study a detailed map of the area that you plan to hunt in (usually something like Google maps). This can be used to look for nearby water, specific trees, hills, elevation and so on.

This can help you narrow down your search, or enhance it. For example, some mushrooms may tend to grow over/under a certain elevation, on hills and/or in association with certain trees and plants. It's also good to map everything out so you don't get lost if you head deep into the woods and lose cell phone service.

So next we will look at some of these locations that are ideal to hunt. But we'll also take a look specifically at some trees and plants, before covering some of the most expensive species of mushrooms that can be found in North America. However, before moving forward, I will state the obvious— you should try to aim your mushroom hunts for days where it has rained recently.

Keep in mind; in the mushroom world, the heavier the rain, the greater the possibilities. But morning dew and fog can work too, so if there hasn't been much rain you can still head out. Sometimes you'll be surprised what is still growing from the last rain! If you're good enough, some foragers report making up to $200/hour. After all, some of these wild mushrooms have a pretty hefty price tag.

This is a map of the Appalachian mixed mesophytic forests, which is an ecoregion within the United States. The climate varies from humid continental (in the Northern section) to humid subtropical (in the southern section). This weather shift occurs near the extreme southern section of Ohio. In 1805, French botanist Francois Andre Michaux wrote that he's travelled all across North America, but has yet to find anywhere else that could compare to the (Ohio Valley) for the "vegetative strength of its forests".

In Appalachia, there may be as many as 20,000 different species of mushrooms that grow wild, (with roughly only 2,500 being identified). The southern section of Appalachia has the larger variety of fungi, and also has the longest potential seasons for them to grow (compared to the northern section).

Appalachia is home to some of the most diverse selection of plants, fungi and animals found in any temperate forests in the world. The ecoregion is usually compared to that of Eastern China.

In Appalachia, the elevation can change drastically, seemingly instantly (as seen in the image above). In the eastern section of Ohio (near Pennsylvania and West Virginia) the gentle rolling hills merge into the Appalachian mountains.

In Columbiana County, Ohio (where most of these images were taken) the elevation can change from 652 ft along the Ohio River, to 1,446 ft at Round Knob— that's a difference of nearly 800 ft! This is largely due to the glacial boundary from the most recent ice age running directly through the county.

The image above is a classic look in Northern Appalachia. This is also an ideal environment for wild mushrooms of many different types of fungi to grow. Several important boxes are checked here, for example; the Appalachian mixed mesophytic forest offers plenty of shade throughout the day— and the borders of the creeks are often lined with plenty of Eastern Hemlock trees. Ferns and numerous different types of other small green plants usually make up the forest ground cover.

This is another example of what an ideal mushroom-hunting environment looks like. The Appalachian forests can provide countless examples, but this one is important. Eastern Hemlock trees line the borders, while ferns again cover the ground. The elevation changes drastically. These rolling hills are always great spots to find wild mushrooms, but more-specifically focus on the hilltops. Valley fog also helps, and is common in the Fall, which you can see in the background.

This path leads to a very rural graveyard—
which is incredibly important to one of my
favorite discoveries yet in the mushroom world
(which I will detail later in the book). These
rural cemeteries are a true hotbed for fungi
of many different types, and there are many
reasons for this. In fact, there are so many
reasons that I wrote a small book about it titled
Mushrooms of the Grave. However, when it
comes to prized mushrooms that you wish to
sell and/or consume, it is best to not pick any
from the actual graveyard. But don't fret,
because this information will still prove to be
of use— as I will demonstrate next.

After searching for wild mushrooms in state
parks, forests, bike trails etc., I eventually

found myself looking through rural graveyards after reading reports of people finding strange mushrooms in these areas. Now, keep in mind with the aforementioned locations— always look into any rules and restrictions that they may have (as each state has different rules as to where you can legally forage).

The main discovery that I made in these graveyards is the Vinca minor plant (aka periwinkle). This plant is an invasive species that was introduced to the United States as ornamental ground cover, and it was widely grown in cemeteries (sometimes as a way to mark unmarked graves where there was no stone).

This would usually occur in the southern parts of the United States, but I've found this plant in graveyards as far north as Ohio. Many mycorrhizal fungi attach to the roots of these plants, but none more noticeable than the Golden Chanterelles— which I'll cover next, before moving on to some other prized edible mushrooms.

In the two images above, I show one of the most important plant species that I've found so far that closely associate with prized mushrooms; Vinca minor (aka periwinkle). Chanterelles in particular, but likely Morels and many other types of mushrooms, will connect to the roots of this invasive ground cover.

With the picture on the left, you can see a very clear, detailed image of what the plant looks like precisely. In the picture on the right, you can see the invasive nature of the species, as it has covered large areas of the forest.

Here, you can see golden Chanterelle
mushrooms growing symbiotically with
Vinca minor. But not only do they grow
well with these plants, they spread throughout
the forest like the invasive species that
they attached to.
I feel that this plant will be of great importance
in future mushroom greenhouse-grows on
a commerical level. Some of these exotic
mushrooms that have yet to be cultivated
(like Amanita muscaria and the variants)
may be possible to grow with this plant (in
my opinion), if done correctly.

After finding a hotspot for fungi, you'll likely become very shocked to see hundreds (if not thousands) of clusters of Golden Chanterelle mushrooms. So, if you can find a rural graveyard where Vinca minor happens to be planted, and check the nearby woods, you will likely find your hotspot.
With just a tiny bit of luck, the periwinkle plant will have spread throughout the woods like the invasive nature of the species. If this has happened, and the weather permits, you should see Golden Chanterelles about every 10-20 feet. They tend to grow best in Summer through Fall.

Golden Chanterelle mushrooms are a species that tend to grow in rather large clusters from Spring through Fall. Usually if you find one, you'll find quite a bit more nearby. They are mycorrhizal, and they usually form a symbiotic relationship with certain trees, such as; beech, maple, oak, birch and poplar. But they seem to especially enjoy growing near moss and also near small green plants and forest ground cover, where they attach to the roots. Price: $48/lb (fresh)

This is two examples of the Honey Fungus
(Armillaria mellea) mushrooms growing at
the base of Oak trees (which is where they
are oftentimes found). "Honey Fungus" is
actually more of an umbrella term, being used
to describe numerous different species and
subspecies of edible mushrooms (usually
belonging to the Armillaria genus).
In North America, these mushrooms typically
fruit in late Summer and throughout most of
the Fall. Honey mushrooms are parasitic, and
they usually attack the roots of living trees.
These mushrooms are usually fairly easy to
spot just by walking a hiking trail for a mile
or two during the right seasons.

Honey mushrooms (as I've previously mentioned) are parasitic and can be found quite often attacking the roots of Oak trees. But broadleaf trees in general are a likely host to this fungus, and the mushrooms do tend to grow in rather large clusters (making them ideal for foraging). In North America, September and October will be primetime for these Honey mushrooms. You also shouldn't have too hard of a time finding them, if you keep your eyes on the base of the trees. Price: $20/lb (fresh)

Above is an example of "Shrimp-of-the-woods" or more technically, Entoloma abortivum. This is an odd species, because some mycologists suggests that this parasitic fungus forms as some sort of reaction to growing near Honey mushrooms and/or parasitizing them. Honey mushrooms usually grow near trees, whereas Shrimp-of-the-woods can be found growing on leaf litter, and even loose dirt in the forest. I found these in abundance near a creek in Ohio, in mid-October.
Price: $28/lb (fresh)

Artomyces pyxidatus, aka the crown-tipped Coral fungus. These mushrooms are quite common and can be found growing on dead wood, specifically from hardwood trees. Coral mushrooms are a species that I come across the very often. They can be found throughout Spring, Summer and Fall— serving as a primary decomposer in the woods. A distinctive feature is their crown tips, (hence the name) which should distinguish it from lookalikes. Price: $20/lb (fresh)

Grifola frondosa, aka Hen-of-the-woods—
these mushrooms grow in late Summer and
into the Fall, and can usually be found
growing at the base of Oak trees. They almost
look like a bouquet of flowers sticking out,
and should basically be in one piece when you
pull it. A lookalike to these mushrooms are
Meripilus sumstinei, which stains black and is
also edible. These mushrooms can usually be
found growing in the same spot for several
years, so keep that in mind if you find a batch.
Price: $18/lb (fresh)

Ganoderma tsugae, aka Reishi Lingzhi: This species of mushrooms has incredible medicinal potential and purposes— being highly sought after by hunters. Their distribution range is rather limited, covering only Asia, South Pacific, Southern Europe, and the Eastern United States. When this mushroom is young it has a very bright appearance, with colors ranging from a whitish-yellow, to orange and red— descending in that order towards the base, becoming duller with age.
They can become quite large and are found primarily in June and July, and sometimes in the Fall, typically growing in Eastern Hemlock forests. Price: $20/lb (fresh)

Turkey Tail Fungus, aka Trametes versicolor is a very common fungus found year round. This fungus has a lot of medicinal potential, as it's currently being studied for it's possible anti-cancer properties. This multicolored bracket fungus typically grows on dead wood, and can sometimes be confused with the false Turkey Tail. A key identifier is the backside of the fungus, where the true Turkey Tail will have visible tube-like pores, whereas the false Turkey Tail will be fairly smooth.
Price: $60/lb (dried)

There a 3 types of the Lion's Mane fungus that grows in the United States, with the above image being Hericium coralloides (coral tooth). The main difference basically being the length of the spines, with the other two species have much larger spines. Lion's Mane are not very abundant in North America, but they can be found in dead, or injured, hardwood trees in late Summer through Fall. The fresh white appearance will turn yellow with age.
Price: $32/lb (fresh)

Here are two examples of Chicken-of-the-woods (Laetiporus sulphureus) mushrooms growing; On the left, you can see a close-up of just how magnificent these mushrooms are while they are still fresh. The large clusters and bright orange glow, are an undeniable natural beauty that can be spotted several hundred yards away.

These mushrooms will usually be spotted growing on dead, or injured oak trees in the Summer and Fall. They are amongst the easiest mushrooms to find, due to their bright orange, glowing appearance. On the right, you can see them fully decomposing a downed tree.

Chicken-of-the-woods mushrooms may enjoy growing on oak trees the most, but they can also be spotted growing on other hardwood trees and even the occasional pine trees (although it is usually recommended not to eat mushrooms growing on conifers). These mushrooms usually grow in large clusters (sometimes several fresh pounds on one tree) and will oftentimes grow on the same tree, over-and-over again until it's full decomposed. Price: $32/lb (fresh)

Old-Man-of-the-woods is an edible mushroom species that is truly special, with it's dark gray/black pyramid-shaped scales on the cap, and it's sweet smell. But one of the most unique features of this species is that it prefers to grow in low mountain ranges (1,000-5,000ft), with them rarely being spotted growing in lowlands (less than 660ft). They also tend to grow on hills, which is the case with this image. Found in the Summer in N. America and Europe. Price: $28/lb (fresh)

Black Morel mushrooms have a tendency to grow where the ground was recently disturbed; e.g; a flood or wildfire. This is precisely why large-landowners will rent a property that was recently burned in a wildfire to Morel hunters to turn a profit from an otherwise not-so-good situation. This species, unlike like their golden Morel counterparts, seems to grow well near pine trees where the soil is slightly acidic and can be found in the Spring.
Price: $44/lb (fresh)

The Pearl Oyster mushrooms are
typically not too hard to find growing in
the wild in Appalachia, as they serve as
one of the primary decomposers of
broadleaf trees (especially Oak). The
growing season will usually extend from
Spring through Fall.
These mushrooms have an
oyster-shaped cap (hence their name)
and a seafood-like flavor and aroma.
Pleurotus Ostreatus is the species used
in the image above. Price: $12/lb (fresh)

Giant Puffball mushrooms are a species
that if you're lucky, you don't even have to
leave your yard to find. They are basically
impossible to miss, because they resemble
a big, white ball and grow in open fields.
They don't necessarily have much taste, but
are great to cook with to absorb other
flavors. Some people use the mushroom to
make pizza dough. These mushrooms grow
in the Summer and Fall, and they can grow
very big (possibly up to 40lbs).
Price: $20/lb (fresh)

Parasol mushrooms (Macrolepiota procera)
are a very unique looking species that
can be found growing in rather large
clusters. In late Summer and early Fall,
you can likely find them growing under
pine trees, especially Spruce.
In fact, I've noticed that they grow in
almost an identical habitat to Amanita
muscaria var guessowii. I've found these
species coexisting within a few dozen
feet on numerous occasions. In the image
above, you can see the very distinct ring
on the stem.

In Appalachia, Parasol mushrooms are typically found from late Summer through Fall (especially under pine trees). They usually grow singly, but oftentimes within ten feet or so you'll see several more in any direction (forming small-to-large groups). Many people claim that this is one of the best-tasting mushrooms in the world, and is highly sought after by many chefs. These mushrooms can get rather large, in height and weight.
Price: $15/lb (fresh)

Auricularia auricula-judae, aka Jelly Ear [or Judas's Ear]. These mushrooms can be found nearly year-round, and grow in small-to-large clusters on fallen dead wood— especially broadleaf trees. They are fairly common, and although they aren't traditionally sold, new research shows that these mushrooms may have a lot of medicinal properties. They are considered edible, but usually not choice. Browsing the forest floor for decaying logs and branches should be sufficient in finding this species of fungus that resembles human ears.

There are more than 400 different types of
Cordycep mushrooms that grow wild, with at
least 10 that grow in North America.
Pictured above, is an image of Cordycep
militaris (which is the most widespread).
Unlike Cordycep sinensis (which only grows
at elevations of 11,500 ft and above in Tibet
and sells for up to an incredible $140,000/lb
dried) these mushrooms sell for significantly
less, but wild Cordyceps can't quite be
replicated, so they still sell for a pretty penny.
Price: Between $500-$1,000/lb (dried)

Next, I'm going to cover a very important mushroom genus; Amanita muscaria (more specifically their variants). In Appalachia, two different variants of this species can be found; first the Amanita muscaria var guessowii (bright orange/yellow cap with white warts). Second, the Amanita persicina (which is known as the "peach-colored fly agaric).

Now the reasons that these species of mushrooms are important are many, but the main reason being they are the only legal hallucinogenic mushrooms that grow wild in North America. The chemicals that the mushrooms contain (muscimol, ibotenic acid and muscarine) are not regulated at all by the FDA, meaning they are all completely legal. However ibotenic acid is technically poisonous and a neurotoxin, so extreme caution must be used. I do not recommend consuming these mushrooms without proper education.

These mushrooms are admittedly a challenge to find, as you have to plan your hunt accordingly with the season, as the season for them is relatively short and complex (even more so in the north). If you want to find these mushrooms, especially in abundance, then there is no place better to recommend than a forest that is dominated by Spruce trees.

Amanita muscaria mushrooms have a long history in North America, which author R. Gordon Wasson has noted in an article that was published in 1957. In the article, Wasson talks about the mention of going to "heaven" after consuming the mushrooms in a letter sent from a Superior of the Jesuit Order, Pére Charles l'Allemant (who was living in Quebec, Canada) to his brother in France. Wasson would later go on to say that with "certainty" the mushrooms discussed were "Amanita muscaria".

Citation: Wasson RG. Traditional use in North America of Amanita muscaria for divinatory purposes. J Psychedelic Drugs. 1979 Jan-Jun;11(1-2):25-8. doi: 10.1080/02791072.1979.10472088. PMID: 392115.

So with the first documented usage of Amanita muscaria being linked to Quebec, Canada, it's likely safe to assume that the mushrooms were in fact variants of Amanita muscaria— as the classic red cap with warts is isolated to the west coast in N. America. So, some of the earliest mushrooms being used as an intoxicant might've been the Amanita muscaria var guessowii.

In the same article, he reports that evidence is also available that indicates American Indian tribes used Amanita muscaria mushrooms for divinatory purposes. Not much research has been conducted about the effects of these specific varieties, along with their habitat and possibilities of cultivating them. This is why I decided to go into much further detail about these special mushrooms in a separate book, titled, The Legal Magic Mushrooms of North America: A Study of the Amanita muscaria Varieties (which I highly recommend reading before going any further with them).

Amanita muscaria var guessowii mushrooms grow in the Fall and are technically poisonous (if unprepared) and hallucinogenic. These mushrooms can only be found in Eastern North America, as they are a variant to the more widespread Amanita muscaria. They are associated with pine trees, specifically Spruce. Because they are hallucinogenic (and have other medicinal properties) they are highly sought after, and legal to possess/sale. Price: $320/lb (dried caps)

Amanita persicina, aka Peach-colored Fly Agaric: Amanita persicina is a type of mushroom that was originally classified as Amanita muscaria, although recent DNA tests suggest that it's better fit as it's own unique species. This species grows most often in Fall, but can be found nearly year-round in some states. The mushrooms are found in Eastern United States— from Florida to Southern and Eastern Ohio, and as far west as Oklahoma. Found in Eastern Ohio, these mushrooms also contain the poisonous and hallucinogenic drugs ibotenic acid and muscimol. Usually not considered edible unless extreme caution is used.

Goodyera pubescens, aka downy rattlesnake plantain. This is a very interesting looking plant that is known to participate in extremely high fungi activity. So they grow very well with mushrooms, and they also grow well in a mostly-shade environment. This plant [orchid] produces flowers which bloom between the months of July and September. This plant is native to Eastern North America, and should be more well-known in the mushroom community— they are common at higher elevations. American Indians would use this plant for medicinal purposes.

Many mushrooms that you find will not be edible, although only roughly 3% of all wild mushrooms in the world are poisonous. So there is no need to have too much fear with wild fungi, but instead approach nature with common sense and some basic understanding. Now, one thing that is always noticeable in the mushroom world, is color advertising (advertising in biology).

Color advertising is basically a living organism's way of attracting, or repelling other organisms. So usually when you see a bright colored plant (or in the case of this book a bright colored mushroom) then you can usually guarantee it's trying to tell you something. For example; with Amanita muscaria, the drugs ibotenic acid and muscimol are supposedly responsible for the coloring on the cap.

Well, the same can also be said for deadly mushrooms, such as the Amanita bisporigera species. This mushroom, which is commonly referred to as the "Eastern Destroying Angel" is bright white— and contains more than a lethal dose of Amatoxins in a single mature mushroom. **Do Not Consume!**

Pictured above are a few images of the Eastern Destroying Angel (the deadliest mushroom in North America). These mushrooms are unfortunately incredibly common, and can usually be seen growing near prized mushrooms. This shouldn't be an issue, unless they're growing on top of each other. However, never put an Eastern Destroying Angel in your bag that you collect other mushrooms in that you plan on consuming. One of the most noticable features, is the remnants of the universal veil left behind (near the base) and the delicate ring near the top of the stem.

Since the Eastern Destroying Angel is such a deadly and common mushroom, I will detail them a bit further. In the image on the left, you can see the universal veil clearly intact (after some careful digging). Prior to the digging, the veil was completely buried underground.
In the image on the right, you can see just how delicate the ring, or skirt (however you wish to describe it) on the upper stem is. This is precisely why extreme caution should be used, because these identifiers may be diminished, or even non-existent. One that should always remain, is the large sac-like volva that you will notice if you dig it up.

In the two images above, are examples of the Jack-o'-lantern mushrooms. These bright orange mushrooms are important to know how to identify, that way you don't confuse them with other orange mushrooms (like Chanterelles or Chicken-of-the-woods).
In the image on the left, is Omphalotus olearius (which grows singularly, or in small clusters and has true gills). In the image on the right, is the Omphalotus illudens (Eastern Jack-o'-lantern) which grows in larger clusters and contains the drug muscarine. The gills of both species can glow in the dark. Both considered toxic.

In the two images above, you can see a quite clear distinction between the true gills of the Jack-o'-lantern mushroom (on the left) compared to the lines under the cap of the Golden Chanterelle (on the right). If you take your finger and swipe across the gills of the Jack-o'-lantern, they will move with ease. However the lines on the Chanterelle mushroom will not budge without force. Also, the Chanterelle mushroom's underside will not glow in the dark, and the orange color in general is usually paler— and Chanterelles are generally funnel-shaped.

As I've previously mentioned, the majority of mushrooms are not edible or poisonous— but that doesn't mean that they should be ignored. Some of the most amazing-looking mushrooms in the world fall into this category, and they still play an equally large part in the fungi kingdom. So, if you want to find exotic-looking mushrooms to take pictures of to show off on the internet, or are just generally curious in finding them, then rest assured late summer is primetime.

This is when a lot of color comes into the mushroom season, and a lot of cool mushrooms that belong to the Amanita genus as well [many Amanita mushrooms are poisonous, and some very deadly]. These mushrooms truly thrive in the hot season, and they can frequently be found growing in the cool shade on the hottest days.

You may want to keep some bug spray handy while adventuring into the woods this time of the year, as they do get very bad. Some of these colorful mushrooms that I will highlight do have uses however, such as in some cases making color dye for art. But even if they had no use at all to man, their visual appeal alone is enough to be intriguing.

I highly advise **not** eating any of the mushrooms and/or plants that I'm going to show next, as I am only sharing them for their visual uniqueness. I also wanted to highlight how some of these mushrooms were actually first described in Ohio— more specifically the Amanita flavorubens, aka Yellow American Blusher. All of these mushshrooms are incredible to look at and photograph, and you can actually still turn a profit if you take good, quality images and sell them.

Other than the different types of Amanita mushrooms, I also wanted to highlight some colorful mushrooms that are quite common in the tri-state area [OH-WV-PA]. Among these colorful mushrooms are my personal favorite to look at, Cortinarius iodes [purple mushrooms]. I found a batch of these purple mushrooms that grow in one single spot on top of a hill for roughly a month straight [August]. Although I've read that some people report consuming them, **I recommend not eating any of these mushrooms!**

These are some of the common Amanita mushrooms found in Appalachia— keep in mind the Amanita genus contains the deadliest mushrooms in the world, so just because these may look cool, never mix them in a bag if you plan on eating others that are mixed with it. When it comes to cross-contamination, you never want to take even the slightest risk.

Now once again, keep in mind that although these mushrooms are colorful and actually quite mesmerizing to look at, that's where it should end. Do not try to defy odds and be a risk-taker. Some of these mushrooms may even be listed as edible in some field guides; such as the above photographed Butyriboletus frostii and Retiboletus ornatipes— but being unknown and/or debated is risky, so it's best to only have a look, in my opinion.

The image on the left is
Actaea pachypoda, aka the white baneberry.
The image on the right is Arisaema triphyllum,
aka the Jack-in-the-pulpit. I find these types
of plants of importance while looking for
fungi, as I've frequently spotted them in close
proximity. Both, the plants and mushrooms
grow well in partial-to-full shade and regular
water. Although some American Indians
would use plants like these for different
medicinal purposes, do not even consider
consuming these plants— as they are
extremely poisonous.

Well, hopefully this book has helped you better understand the mushroom world— and the possibilities of profit that can be accomplished within it. But even more importantly, if you do plan on foraging for these wild mushrooms, that you do so in a respectful manner. This means using the correct onion-sack style bag (so the spores can drop and new mushrooms can grow) while collecting. This also means not foraging where it's against the law, or forbidden.

Please do not use this book as a guide to consuming mushrooms, this was for documentation and educational purposes only!

Thank you for reading!

More books from Author;

The Legal Magic Mushrooms of North America: A Study of the Amanita muscaria Varieties

Mushrooms of the Grave

How to Grow Psilocybin Mushrooms

Psychedelic Drugs and the Ultimate Pursuit for Mind Control

Last of a Dying Breed: An Up-Close Look at the Final Stages of Outlaw Country Music